Beach Glass

Finding New Beauty
in What Survives the Storm

· · · · · · · · · · · · · · · · · · · ·

Linda Haffner Binley

Published by Linda Haffner Binley. Linda@LindaBinley.com

The conversations and events in this book all come from the author's recollections, though they are not written to represent word-for-word transcripts. Rather, the author has retold them in a way that evokes the feeling and meaning of what was said. In all instances, the essence of the dialogue is accurate. In certain cases, events were written about long after their occurrence and circumstances have changed (legal access to certain beaches, for example). The author has written as she recalls best of that time and place, accurate to her memory.

For information about special discounts available for bulk purchases, sales promotions, fundraising and educational needs, contact Linda@LindaBinley.com.

Book formatting and cover(s) design by Joel Pritchard.
Cover photograph by Linda Binley. All rights reserved.
Original artwork by Salem Cade. All rights reserved.

This book is typeset in Palatino Linotype and Run Wild.

Visit the author's website at www.LindaBinley.com.

ISBN-13: 978-1-7332341-0-8

Table of Contents

Dedication

For my own "maggie and milly and molly and may:"
my precious Rachel, Maria and Lena, and my beloved Wade.

As E. E. Cummings said,
"it's always ourselves we find in the sea."
Indeed, we did, and also each other.

·1·

Salt Creek

My girls are still sleeping at home, and Wade surfs the point. This early morning May air has a chill to it, but every onshore gust rolling off the ocean hints of the buttery warm day ahead. The silvery rims of my footsteps behind me reflect impossible sky colors for the second they linger before disappearing back into the flat wet sand. So much of the beauty here flees before it can be captured and quantified; I am amazed at the ridiculous generosity of this place. It reminds me of some fictional stunning woman completely unaware of her beauty, carelessly setting into motion a hundred hearts and a hundred novels with one accidental lock of hair straying across her mermaid eyes.

I have on my most slobbish pair of sweats and a castoff sweatshirt I dug out of the give-away bag, only slightly torn at its front pocket. I know I brushed my teeth, but don't recall grooming my hair before lassoing it into this ponytail. Were my youngest daughter awake, she never would have let me out of the house like this. But here today I am perfect. I am not fleet like the runners passing me by, but I do love them and smile at their efforts. I share the joy of the surfers playing in the water; their happy calls to each other include me. Even the expensive homes crowding the bluff to my right, the Ritz Carlton hotel behind me, and the still-folded umbrellas set out for the beach-going guests of the Monarch Beach Resort charm me today; we all excitedly crowd in together to take our places in this day like musicians in an orchestra. Our conductor warms up before us, tapping out notes of pinks and aquas and whites, alerting us to the symphony ahead.

Part of my glee in this day lies in the bounty at my feet: nearly every step reveals another piece of beach glass, and not just the little browns and greens. In fact, I am skipping over those tiny shards that would usually delight me to scoop up the veritable hunks I practically stub my toes on. Ambers, jades, cobalts – any one of these would make my day all by itself, and this morning, my sweatshirt pouch is rapidly filling with any number of them. Extravagant, lavish bounty; I feel like stopping one of these runners just to point out the ore I am mining – look at this! Look at this! Do you understand what an epic day this is? But I just smile to myself and keep stuffing my finds into my own torn pouch. I am a dumpy millionaire glass slob, giggling at how unbelievably rich I am with treasure.

I come to the runoff separating the public beach from the portion in front of the gated community of Monarch Bay. Technically still public sand and water, but with this deep runoff keeping most shod runners and walkers back, it acts almost private. I, however, gluttonously wade through and take my extra portion of beach today. When I have to take a little leap to get over a deeper part of the runoff, my overfull pouch actually spills out a few of my prized pieces of beach glass, which I bend to retrieve. As I stand again, I see a familiar shape jogging towards me on her own travel down this strand of sand. It is Natalie, my oldest daughter's good friend.

Natalie is fresh-scrubbed and awake, on a weekend break from UCLA, where she majors in psychobiology. That serious focus of study sounds almost incongruous to her postcard looks: she is nearly six feet tall, dark blonde and blue-eyed, lightly freckled. She is one of those stunning girls unaware of her beauty, which has already broken several hearts, puzzling her. Her year at school has been brutally difficult and demoralizing. Playing in the big leagues now, she fights for every grade against all the other top students who earned their way into UCLA. The curve is not her friend. As we chat, I can see her fatigue, her shaken confidence. I also notice that she has lost weight, and I hope that she is healthy.

She describes her year so far, her happiness to be home this weekend, her appreciation for her high school beach. She is smiling, but there are tears behind her words, tears of doubt that she is enough, that she will succeed enough to progress to the next step in her career path and be accepted into graduate school. Based on her grades so far, she is considering downshifting her aspirations. She is nineteen.

I reach into my pouch. Without looking, my fingers select three large pieces of my treasure. I take Natalie's hand and give her an aqua, a white, and a lime green piece of this day's sea glass. I don't even remember what I say, only what I want to say: You are enough. You are perfect. God will tumble you a bit on the way down your path, just to take off the newness, but you are already shining so beautifully. Don't be afraid; what you will lose is so much less important than the refined part of yourself that will be left. Take your unique place in your glorious life that is a part of this day and be at peace.

Although each is a treasure, the three pieces of beach glass are not enough. I cannot truly give her what I would like to give her. I would like to scoop out a portion of what it has taken me decades to learn for myself: knowing that amongst the doubts is the person that has every right to be here, and dream the biggest dreams she wants to dream. I would like to empty out Natalie's pouch

14

of herself, editing from her treasure the jagged pieces of glass that drive her to compare herself and conclude that she is any "less than." I would like to replace those shards with some truly gorgeous specimens from my own pouch, like the one which reveals new dreams, the piece that allowed me to see that trading out my first dreams for new ones was part of the process, that getting my sharp corners tumbled off to reveal a new shape was part of the plan all along. Had my beach glass remained a bottle, or a windshield, or a marble, it would have never become a treasure. Shiny and new has its season, but it is impossible to stay that way, unless you would stay in the box you came in, stowed on a closet shelf, away from life itself. Any collector of fine beach glass knows that the best pieces require first a break, and then a lot of tumbling along the way.

We hug and say goodbye. Natalie says that she will keep the beach glass on her desk at school and remember our talk this day whenever she sees it. I watch her run south towards the surf point and the busier part of the beach, her ponytail swinging back and forth in time to her strides.

My moment with her lingers, its unique tone a balancing note in the music of this morning. My hands are buried up to the wrists in my pouch, smoothing the rounded corners of glass between my fingers like prayer beads. I silently ask for a woman on a beach for each of my daughters, knowing that many of their future low moments will happen without me, that their own tumbling is inevitable and painful, and that I cannot protect them from it. They will not see their real beauty yet, emerging from a chrysalis that is already lovely, but which must be broken open for them to truly materialize. It is a necessary process, yet I would give all my bounty to them to protect them from the pain of it.

I turn back to finish my walk to the north end of the beach. Ahead is the little cove we have named "Secret Beach," which I will only be able to reach if I pick over a longish curved stretch of large rocks. Sometimes I find special pieces of beach glass there along the way, wedged between the boulders. I will also look for coffee beans, the rare *Trivia californiana* shells my husband and I have found up and down this coast to the tip of

Baja. Most often, though, I merely find pieces of glass that are not ready for me that I will throw back into the breaking waves to find me another day and bless the little hike it took to reach them.

The beauty of this early day still envelops me. I perform my piece in this symphony, too, somewhere between the high notes gleefully singing out over the water, and the downbeat of the waves sucking back out after breaking. It is an aqua day, and I am aqua in it.

• 2 •

West Street

This is Char's beach. Nearly every day begins with her descent down these steep musty stairs under the renegade bamboo to reach the deep sand here, to walk the length of this beach. She sometimes even walks around the cliffs at its north point to reach Aliso Beach, which has its own adjacent parking lot, and is therefore easily reached and a world away in mood from this more secluded beach. West Street remains a "local" spot, with a combination of skimboarders, readers, walkers and volleyballers each claiming their piece of it. The beach sand is deep and white, and usually a berm forms, separating the fluffier dry sand from the wet strip at the water's edge. Towards the south end, tidepools swirl in the rocks, and in the summer, deep pools result where bikinied mothers take their tots by the hand and protectively teach them about the power of the waves, shielded from the breakers by the reef.

Char is my grave competition, and if I am completely truthful, she has me vanquished. Throughout her home, jars and bottles, boxes and drawers strain with her lifetime stash of beach glass. Sunlight streaming through her windows lights up her home like a kaleidoscope, the multitude of beach glass in containers refracting the light as a million prisms. One might expect her to be careless with such a quantity, but Char delights still in every piece. She has been generous when asked for beach glass to decorate a wedding or needed for a craft, but her generosity belies the value she still puts on her bounty.

Besides her morning walks, Char's days include volunteering in the classrooms of her elementary school teaching friends, acting as a docent at Sherman Gardens in nearby Corona Del Mar, swimming miles at the YMCA, and handcrafting beautiful beaded jewelry. She keeps in touch with her children, to whom she is a single mom. Her son attends UCLA, and her oldest daughter is working her way through the Colombia School of Law, after having graduated from Stanford. Her younger daughter, her middle child, has created a career out of her fashion training to become the wardrobe director for a Shakespearean theater troupe in London, England, where she directs the handcrafting and stewardship of historically and thematically correct costumes.

I have traveled with Char to Florida, and frolicked with her locally many times, as we are both members of the Oyster Tribe, our book club group of friends (emphasis on "club," not "book"). Usually by the time I have finished my first morning cup of tea at one of our trips or overnight Christmas parties, she has ticked off two or three activities in her day and is in the middle of a randy story of her latest dating escapade. She has danced me under the table more than once, and her "death drop" shimmies are the stuff of legend. She has fearlessly trawled the waters of the internet dating sites and warns that the commercials on television only portray the dozen or so normal men that were ever members. Still, she courageously ventures forth (although her latest date may be taking her off the market, as he keeps annoyingly, and romantically, sailing her off into sunsets on his yacht).

Frankly, Char fatigues me. Her daily achievements highlight my own sloth, and my waste of the many hours granted me. Did I not love and admire her, I would probably slap her. To be honest, because she stays so active, she would probably retaliate by soundly beating me, and I would be a fool to challenge her. So actually, I guess I wouldn't slap her.

Did I mention that Char traveled to Florida with a spray bottle of water? Or that she had to go through a special line at the airport security check? The water was to spray her feet when her daily pain reached its hot zenith in the humidity of the Keys. The special security line was because she needs to explain the electronic device surgically embedded in her back. It continuously sends out impulses to interrupt those of her own nervous system, which sends constant pain signals from her brain to her body. On any given day, Char's pain level registers at an unceasing, burning, 7-9 out of 10 (many days escalating to 10), no matter what pain medication she takes. She has Reflex Sympathetic Dystrophy (RSD).

When Char was a girl, her exceedingly high foot arches regularly ached, prompting her parents to entrust her to a surgeon, who cut into Char's feet, dissembling the bones and tissue there, and artificially flattened out her arches. As with many sufferers of RSD, this surgery acted as the inciting factor setting off a lifetime of severe and unrelenting pain, through a chronic malfunction of her nervous system. Char's pain began in her feet, and is still most intensely concentrated there, but also marches throughout her body, having continually advanced upward over the years. Although 200,000 – 1.2 million Americans (mostly women) suffer from RSD, it is commonly misdiagnosed. The typical RSD patient sees five doctors before an accurate diagnosis, including psychiatrists, since sufferers are often told it is all "in their heads."

You can ask Char about any of this, if you can catch her. Among the rest of her activities, you may find her on the phone with another RSD sufferer, since she peer-counsels many, lending her shoulder and encouragement to anyone in crisis. RSD bears the unfortunate distinction of having the highest suicide rate of any chronic disease among its sufferers, a statistic Char works to correct. You could ask her about the disease if you want to, and I'm sure she would informatively lay out all the facts. She might explain that it is West Street's uniquely uncompacted sand which cushions her fragile feet that makes it her favorite beach, and that her busy mornings bear witness to her knowledge that her pain will peak later, so she seizes as much life as possible before noon. Probably, however, she will ask you about your kids, whose names she has remembered, or tell you about the next trip she is planning. If you are a collector, she will glance around before settling back into a soft cushion and whispering about her latest beach glass find. The world around will fade away, as together you will nod over the injustice of a mutual friend (amateur and casual collector) finding a huge perfectly smoothed shard of red glass, just minutes after Char had completed her beach walk in the same spot.

Hanging in my home, I have a mobile constructed of driftwood hung with fishing line. From each strand of line dangles precious beach glass and shells, accented by crystal beads. The beach glass ranges in shade from turquoise and soft blue, to white and various shades of light green, with nary a spot of brown or common Kelly green. Each shard has been hand-drilled to be hung, a process that I know takes a specialized water drill, and considerable hand exertion. There are four strands of line, three of which are approximately eight inches long. The fourth is just three inches long. When I opened this birthday gift, there was a collective gasp in the room, as everyone there (both collector and amateur) appreciated its sheer beauty, and the effort it took to create it. Char took me aside later to apologize for the one short strand, explaining that she just plain ran out of strength before she could complete it, but still wanted to gift it to me on time.

Over the years it has hung in my home, and after all the hours I have spent admiring it, however, I have come to regard that one short strand as my favorite. Anyone can make a perfectly balanced mobile. Anyone can declare "finished" a piece of art that is symmetrical. But my mobile bears the unique stamp of its maker, and no one else could have created it. With all of her strength, Char crafted me this costly work of art, choosing to spend who knows how many of her precious windows of health on me, first finding the glass and then crafting it into its present form. I touch my finger to a strand of it as I pass it during my days, treasuring the beauty of its glass made perfect in brokenness, treasuring the beauty of my friend, reflecting the dazzling light of her life upon me through the prism of her pain.

To learn more about RSD, or to donate, please visit https://rsds.org/

· 3 ·

Table Rock

When our first daughter was a newborn, we would walk down to this beach from our rental house in South Laguna. Usually, she would be cradled into a carrier on her daddy's protective chest. We would also be toting an umbrella, a diaper bag with all her required supplies, possibly dive equipment, towels, food, and probably a beach chair. One of my husband's beach friends nicknamed him "the human pack horse." Traveling with a baby, especially a first born, is about as simple as a pier pulling up stakes and changing location. That applies even when the travel is just across Pacific Coast Highway.

Table Rock is a pocket beach, a hidden

carved out cove that is accessible, like so many beaches in South Laguna, only via a steep staircase. The staircase here is constructed of wood, and doubles back upon itself many turns before delivering the climber to the sand at the bottom of the cliff. At the bottom, you can choose to find an immediate "camp" spot or work your way around the corner to the secondary cove and settle there. Regardless, you will find tall picturesque rock outcroppings in the water, and a beach break so abrupt that the waves seem to paint themselves into seascapes with every dramatic crash.

Our trips here now entail much less gear, as the newborn is nearly twenty, and off onto her own adventures. On a recent summer day, we had only our middle daughter with us, and she quickly separated from us at the bottom of the stairs to stake her own claim at a distance, settling in with a girlfriend and a new collection of magazines, glancing up regularly to check on the gallery of tattoos (and the muscles beneath them) parading by. I know, because I was spying on her, of course.

Usually, however, it is a quick morning walk that brings my husband and me here together, perhaps having stopped at a nearby cafe for a latte to bring along and sip while we hunt out fresh pieces of beach glass to add to our collection. We rarely even bring a beach bag, and since a friendly law enforcement official reminded us one day that dogs are not allowed here, not even the pups. This day, the beach is uncrowded. The two daughters still at home are in school, and we have headed out together on a special Thursday morning island of time.

I am tired and quiet. We talk about nothing in particular on the way down, mostly just bits about the girls, or the business, or whatever we see as we walk. I am nursing a sore foot, and upon arrival I refresh it in the cool water at the north end of the beach. It feels good, and I realize that I don't feel like walking the whole length of the beach, while Wade's own trail of beach glass is taking him down to the other end. It is a peaceable separation, just a quiet and gradual kind of moving apart, realizing that we will meet up again soon. I watch him bob down to pick up a prize, examine it, and either put it in his pocket or toss it back into the water. Up close he does not look his age, and at this distance, he looks like a teenager in his board shorts. I wonder if we will one day be like the celebrity couples in the gossip rags: "she" looking so much older than "he."

The water swirls around my feet, delivering and sucking back portions of the uniquely grainy sand of this beach. Do all little girls like to stand just within the reach of the advancing waves, letting the ocean bury their feet up to the ankles, wiggling just a bit to help get the job done? I revisit being eight, and watch my feet disappear. As I observe this process, I am delighted and surprised to note a few pieces of glass amongst the sand at my feet. They take their places in my jogger pocket, and I begin observing the fruit of the waves more closely. Each wave seems to bring more glass with it, and without really even moving from my spot, my pocket begins to fill.

I am like a safecracker who has discovered the code: just stand still, and the waves will do all the work! As I work my new system, Wade has wound his way back, and joins me in this gleaning process. We stand together at the water's edge, reaching down, sharing the latest piece, advising one who would cheat just a bit to not be greedy and throw back the pieces that are not truly ready (and yes, I did throw them back). A difference in his touch alerts me to look out to sea as a bigger wave starts to break, requiring me to back up for safety. The sun warms us and the water cools us, and the sporadic beach sounds of voices and bird-calls serenade us. We are still talking about noth-ing in particular, just giggling at this surprising process, standing together at the shoreline, point-ed in the same direction.

We stand together in the same place, yet the ocean brings us a new world with every breaking wave. To the observer, it would probably appear that we are not accomplishing much, just two old-ish people standing there picking up stuff every once in a while. Yet our pockets swell with our spoils. Soon it is time to leave, announced by a subtle shift in the light. He reaches for my hand at the same moment I reach for his. I am struck that the victory of this day consisted mostly in simply staying.

We wind our way up the many steps. Some-times, as he did when I was pregnant, my husband gives me a bit of upward pressure at the small of my back, which helps just enough to propel me up the stairs. I never asked him or taught him to do this, yet he knew and still does.

More than two decades unite us, and we have stood at many shorelines. We have discovered many treasures yet had to throw back a few that were less than wonderful. Sometimes, those very same pieces find us later, when we are able to keep them, and when we are no longer cut by their sharp edges. They have smoothed, and we have strengthened.

At various times, I may have desired to keep walking down that beach, as I'm sure he has, too. Yet, we stay. Our paths diverge and reunite, always progressing in the same direction back towards the true north of each other. It is a surprising ache when I realize how much I miss him while he is away, and how much I store up to tell him. He is so different than me. Yet he is my dearest friend. We receive what time brings us, discovering that our treasure has come as the result of, as much as anything, simply staying. Had either of us left after a particularly stormy set of breakers,

I marvel at what we would have missed. This spot we have found is a good spot, a fruitful spot, a mysterious and surprising spot. Our pockets are full as we stand together.

· 4 ·

Crystal Cove

Maria is in third grade, and horribly distressed. Her new teacher this year is mean. Every afternoon brings with it a fresh list of terrors that have unfolded between 8:05 and 2:20. Many days, my girl has had to sit out recess on the stoop because she has not completed her work in the time allotted, and she has to work at a little clipboard while she watches her classmates play. At first, buoyed by our wonderful prior experiences with gifted teachers at our little elementary school, and taking for granted the scholastic and interpersonal success my daughters have had in all of their classes, I side with the teacher, encouraging Maria to "get that work done," to "buckle down and quit wasting time." Then I visit the classroom.

There are posters of consequences on more than one wall for "bad behavior." There are tally marks on the whiteboard, beside the names of children being held accountable for all their transgressions. The "portable" classroom is crowded and messy, and smells stale. Without one interaction there, and knowing that I am an adult, able to leave at any time, I can still feel my stress level rising. The teacher smiles, logically explains all her classroom procedures, and states where my Maria is lacking. But her pointed nails are garishly painted; her hair is long and reminds me of a witch. Every finger has a ring on it; her neck holds four or five necklaces, and the busyness of the room and the person start to make me dizzy.

Because I am a bit of a pill, I ask her where are the posters for positive behavior, and what happens to the kids who do their work expediently? I am beyond listening for her answer because I can already see what is going on here, damn it, and I want my child out. I leave the recess conference and pass several children with clipboards sitting outside the portable. Maria is mercifully out to play this day.

The principal patiently explains that all third-grade classes are full, eliminating the possibility of a move for Maria, no matter how determinedly her mother has marched up to the office. I am so mad and frustrated that I start to cry, which I hate but secretly hope will influence the principal to pull a white rabbit out of her hat. It does not. Alas, my child must stay where she is for the time being.

I stew all night, beyond anger. I am *pissed*. Upon awakening, I resolve that I will NOT take my child back to that classroom, at least for today. Instead, she comes with me for a beach walk with friends at Crystal Cove. One of us has been gifted the use of a "beach house" (mobile home, pre-State Park) by family friends, and is staying there for a while to ease a heart grieving the recent loss of her young husband. We have gathered to walk with her for a bit, because that is about all we can do.

This beach stretches long and wide, terminating to the south at the cliffs of Irvine Cove (where the house we see atop the cliff was reportedly built for heiress Joan Irvine, with a whole round room devoted just to butterflies), and mean-dering north all the way to Corona del Mar, off in the distance. Here, a beach walk could take on the nature of a trek, lasting all day if need be. Today appears to have presented such a need.

We begin as a group, chattering like the sea birds diving and eating around us. There are hugs and some tears, but there are also laughs. We take turns carrying our friend's seven-month old daughter, as the new designation of "widow" is heavy enough burden for her. Maria is the only other child here, with the rest grown up, like her mom. As the little sponge she is, Maria holds my hand and watches these women crying and laugh-ing and holding one another. I hope that she is breathing in great fresh gulps, refreshing herself with this unstale sea air and the love surrounding her.

The line of women begins to spread out in spaced clumps. We are still together, but some are setting a brisker pace, and that clump breaks away north. I can still hear bits of their conversation and read the rest via exuberant body language. I feel confident that several major world problems will be solved there by the time we all reunite. More to the middle, quieter conversation punctuated by gentle nods ensues. Hands are pressed onto arms, and this is where the baby is being passed about. Maria and I peaceably bring up the rear, as we have slowed to begin a treasure hunt of beach glass. I have not come with expectations, but this is one of my all-time favorite hunting grounds, and I have begun to fill my pockets. Perhaps because it has acted as a private enclave for generations of summering families, and the laissez faire remains of their infamous sunset parties make it into the ocean, I have always been lucky here, coming away consistently with gorgeous hunks of beach glass bounty.

Today Maria and I work as a team. I can see the grayness of her stressful school days unknitting itself from her little frame as she discovers and examines, walks and runs, showing me her treasures and appreciating mine. Summer is only newly over, and she is still tan, her particular shade a delicious and creamy latte. She has quickly shed her little sweater and shoes, and the wheat-colored wispies of her hair begin to work themselves out of a barrette.

"Look at this one, Mommy!" Her voice is light and excited, both slowing me down and lifting me up to her pace. We are far from clipboards and tally marks, our bare feet sugaring up as we dip them into the water chasing a treasure, and then digress into the warm dry sand after another. Now we are very far behind all the women. We are both thirsty, and my shoulders feel tightly hot, so we are the first to turn back. Up on the deck, we sort our plunder by color, sipping our water and talking. Maria turns each piece over and over, making piles within the piles, laying whites against each other to discern the faintest tints of blue or green or lavender.

She is a great talker, liberated from both an older and a younger sister today with Mommy to herself. She discusses each decision with me, showing me subtleties I had not noticed. She picks out bits of seaweed and twigs of driftwood, making piles for those, too. Among the talk of color and shape, she weaves mentions of school and babies, and daddies that pass away. We turn each thought over and over, finding a pile for each to fit

45

into, punctuated by quiet looks out onto the rippled sea. We like some pieces of our glass better than others, we like the truth of some of the things we talk about better than others, but we consider each, and find a pile for it as best we can. Even the ocean is more today than it looks like at first glance, and hard to categorize: it is not just blue, but green and white, steel-colored, purple and pink.

By the time the women return, our piles are as scientifically categorized as we can make them. We have organized what we can, and found that some pieces, like some experiences, cannot easily be put into merely one pile. We have decided that some must be returned to the sea, as they are treasures not quite ready for our discovery. It is truly an immense haul. One of my friends exclaims that she and her (older) kids have not found this much sea glass in all their years of looking! Maria smiles, cocking her head onto her shoulder, twisting a strand of her hair, and climbs into my lap. What is her secret, my friend wants to know?

"You have to look," says my child. "You just have to look."

She will return to school after this day, back to the witch's room. Her clipboard days will diminish, however, and we both will make our peace with a difficult situation. We stop fighting what we cannot change, and Maria starts bringing home some happy stories of her days. I would like to say that this teacher becomes her favorite (and mine) and that what she learns in her classroom teaches my child valuable lessons that she takes with her all the days of her life. However, within a few weeks, an opening occurs in a newly formed grade 3/4-combination class, resulting from a twisting Rubik's cube of enrollment numbers, and Maria is moved. This new teacher calls her students "sweet peas" and greets them "good morning" every day at the door with a friendly handshake. She is gentle and loving and positive. We take hold of this treasure, and we never look back.

We put the first part of this third-grade year onto its own pile of experiences. We do not throw it back, but rather keep it, realizing that its color has brought a new richness to Maria's character, a new dimension that strengthens her. But we also put onto our pile our day at Crystal Cove, a tender piece of treasure both bitter and sweet, heavy sorrow made lighter by its weight being shared, endless tears given respite on the shoulders of friends. Sometimes things are hard, and we need to take a break. Sometimes things are hard, and after that break is over, we have to return to them. And sometimes after things are hard, they get better, and we are happier. But we travel through these times together, do our best, and add their colors to our lives, to our piles, diligently looking for the treasure each contains.

· 5 ·
Shaw's Cove

Shaw's Cove is another "local" beach, difficult to find, and, as it is nestled into a residential zone, population-controlled by the near impossibility of finding parking nearby. On a summer day, it looks like a postcard of anyone's version of Laguna: dramatic homes atop cliff sides planted with poker-topped aloe plants, azure water breaking white around the painterly placed rocks just off a curvy beach highlighted with various bright shades of beach towels and umbrellas. It begs for someone in a smock with an easel.

But during the winter storm season, Shaw's presents another face. In these times, the sea tears all the fleshy sand from Shaw's sides, leaving mere tatters of the beach clinging to its rocky bones. Strange and surprising things wash up from the sea, and treasures long forgotten tend to surface. We have come here dodging raindrops, stir-crazy this storm season, with a raging appetite for oxygen. And we find a pirate.

His head down and his hands busy, he doesn't notice us at first. He is quick and decisive with his tools: a tall plastic liquid measuring cup and a huge spoon. He digs and digs, then examines the tailings, focused and clearly in pursuit. He disappears from sight, yet we can still hear him scraping at the wet sand. My girls and I join hands, and step around a boulder. Curiosity fueling our brash courage, we step into his world.

His brown skin evidences a commitment to the beach even in winter, its olive tone confusing his ethnicity and age. His hair is woven from various shades of silver, white and an occasional strand of black. Its deep waves off his forehead tell of a habit of strong and busy hands unconsciously sweeping through it. He is either about ready to go for a haircut or has lately abandoned that convention. His clothes tell me nothing of his character or respectability, and while I consider backing back around the corner I have just rounded with my two little girls and my incipient pregnancy, my five-year-old pipes up: "Are you a pirate?"

He looks up, startled, and my grip tightens. Laguna attracts both lovable eccentrics, and others best enjoyed from afar by a mother with young ones. I prepare to beat a quick retreat if needed. Then he smiles, and we stay.

"A pirate? Why would you say that?"

My oldest daughter is nothing if not observant. "You look like you're digging for treasure."

Whatever he was before this chapter of his life, he is clearly now a pirate. Even if only named as such in this instant, he is a pirate. He looks from his tools to the sand, as if inspecting both the instruments and this concept for the first time. "Well, that's exactly what I am doing. So I guess I am a pirate."

He turns his wrists over and back, and we notice a gold bracelet on each. He pauses before speaking, as if an urge to guard a secret treasure map and an urge to share the tales of his plunder war within him. Braggadocio wins out. "I found both of these here, and this, too." He lifts a thick gold chain from his shirt collar. "Lots of money, too."

He shakes a blue-green coin out of the measuring cup onto the sand. In some previous incarnation it may have been change from an ice cream cone purchase, or telephone money given to a pre-cellular child on his way to this beach without his mother. Its rough asymmetrical edges were surely once round, but are now reshaped by the tumbling of many tides and the layering on of oxidation. Like beach glass, it has been through the ocean's metamorphic process, and come out something different than was originally designed. Perhaps once a dime or a nickel, clearly it is now a doubloon. It is pirate chest treasure, nothing less, and my girls' eyes widen in its hypnotic blue-green glow.

"You can't have that one. But dig around the rocks, and maybe you'll find your own." He has caught the allure of an audience as surely as a virus, and plays up his role, tossing crumbs of advice out as a trail to treasure like his own. The girls look up to me to make sure it's okay, and we soon drop into a teamwork rhythm in this new endeavor, as if searching for buried treasure is what we always do on Tuesdays. Others have also made their way down to Shaw's for saline infusions of the negative ions we are all transfusing by the lungful. But they only glance our way and move on, mapping out their own adventures of the day.

No, he never uses a metal detector, is his patient answer to one of our many questions. Doesn't need one, because he knows where to dig. He points out the backsides of the boulders, explaining to the girls how these rough spots capture his bounty carelessly left behind on a sunny day months or years ago. Or on a passionate night, I silently observe, thinking that a gold necklace such as the one he wears would have been more likely coaxed off by kisses than by a game of smash ball.

I have been to this beach before; in fact, more often before I was married than afterwards. I remember a picnic here, detailed and thoughtfully prepared for me by a date on college break from graduate school in Arizona. I don't remember his name now, just that he told me he shared it with a character in a movie. I can see the prawns he brought, and my hat and my bathing suit, and I can feel myself rising in the waves with him. We laughed, and I'm sure we kissed, and then he went back to school, and we moved on from each other. I turn over the unearthing of that day in my mind's eye, wondering if he wears it as a gold necklace or a bracelet in his own memory. Am I someone's pirate treasure?

The girls scratch and dig, examine their own excavations and compare bounty, discussing merits and value of various finds. They are so marvelously busy at this age, five and three, all their activity punctuated by streams of conversation. Everything is important to them, as they are to each other, and the small envelope of our world contains us sweetly. I know we will be talking about our pirate day through bath time, and that they will later detail all the activities of the dig for their daddy.

The break in the storm looks about to close. While we had our heads down working, the white clouds were being run off the horizon by fat grey ones. We gather each other up and make plans to come back with better tools another day, a day we are sure we will find our own gold bracelet. As we thank our pirate, he shakes out a few blue-green coppery coins for each girl, which are taken with great seriousness and gratitude. Years on, we will find these rough coins among their girl treasures, still smelling of magic. We will recall this day together, and ponder which craggy rock at Shaw's Cove has captured our own essence, stowing it away beneath the sand, to be revealed by some future storm, dug out by some other diligent pirate.

•6•
Treasure Island

It is the first Tuesday after Labor Day, first day of public school, and the ladies are lunching. For years, we have celebrated this day by bringing lunches in boxes and bags, homemade or creatively purchased, for a swap to celebrate the beginning of the school year. Yes, we love our children, and yes, we loved the summers with them around all day, but we still have always been honest enough to recognize the gift in an 8:00am to 2:00pm day without them. Most of our kids are out of high school now, either in college or making their way in careers, but we still set aside this day to celebrate.

Today we meet at Treasure Island, the Montage Beach, having wound our way down through the recently built resort. Before the Montage hotel occupied the bluff above us, Treasure Island claimed it, a private Laguna Beach mobile home park, and the beach still bears its name. Multi-generational families enjoyed this beach as their own summer spot. Today, however, the eBay couple has changed this into a destination for upscale hotel guests, among them the occasional movie star. (A friend of mine once met a young man with an English accent here while walking her dog, someone "really nice, named Orlando or something," and described a person whose face I have seen many times in magazines and on the big screen.)

The water is still the crazy greenish turquoise color it's always been, and the sand is still deep and white. Although the calendar says "school," the heat and the refracting light making me squint says summer. But it is the best secret summer: all the crowds are gone and the weather is still perfect. We set up camp, bumping umbrellas to umbrellas to create maximum shade. This year, we have brought not just lunch, but mojitos on ice. We possess this stretch of the beach virtually by ourselves, at a distance from the hotel's tan umbrellas and khaki attendants. The water is a mojito unto itself, refreshing and thirst-inducing at the same time, teasing us with an impossible color that makes us tip up our sunglasses and take a second look. We will have a swap and a steal of these lunches, as always, and I wonder if anyone prepared a gag lunch as in years past, of tinned Vienna sausage, one lemon, or Ensure.

The laughter starts, our constant. When the kids were younger, we spent many beach hours together, but now that they are older, we sometimes go months without seeing one another. We have much to say, and out-squawk the gulls. The clothes peel off, and the liquid gets poured. We are a more varied group than one would guess from the outside: a nurse, an architect, a photographer, an attorney. A volleyball coach, a realtor, an MBA. Married, divorced, remarried, widowed. We toast the working teachers, both our friends and those with our kids. We are all mothers except for one. Some of us play hooky from jobs, while others have this day off, or are full time moms who work in the home.

Our friendships span many years, enough to have weathered big storms together. Some hurricanes blew from the husband atmosphere: several who preferred substances or other women to wives; a few who died too young. Second husbands. Some typhoons raged from the child climate zone: kids who uplifted our hearts along with themselves as they soared, and took part in Indian Princess, high school sports, college scholarships, the military. Kids who have also broken our hearts, with calls or no calls in the dead of night, and membership in other associations: rehab programs, jail, psychiatric wards, destructive relationships. The children who taught us that those two lists are not mutually exclusive. A child who died.

Some of us are rich, some are poor, and some of us have been both and maybe back again in the space of recent years. Our bodies range from size two to size don't-even-ask. We are battle scarred by cancers removed, breasts added or subtracted, walking canes presently laid aside. We have been broken, inside and out, and put back together in ways we never imagined. But we are here. We are together. We celebrate more than a return of the kids to school: we celebrate our own return to the spectrum of ourselves we see reflected in each others' eyes.

Leslie has worn one of her big-brimmed hats, and a bikini. Out of 15 or so of us staying one year in a funky hotel in Warner Springs, she was the one picked out by the resident sun worshipper, who parted his leathery lizard lips to say, "Hello, Leslie" as she had walked by in her black bikini, gold necklace and black wide-brimmed hat. She is like a magnet to the male species, and to fun of the wild persuasion. She is the one who feeds me alcohol when I need it as an antidote to my own seriousness and leaves magenta lipstick on my wine glasses. Now she gets me out of my chair and into the water, and I know better than to protest.

We are all in the water, playing like dolphins. Our buoyancy silences the various body parts that ail us, and unwanted years drop off as we dive like children under the surf. Char is here. Gentle Patty is here, as is one of the Julies, one of the Hollies, Lynn and Suzanne. Heidi's deep laugh breaks like a wave. She is a labor and delivery nurse, and has delivered many of us from peril: plucked us from the downward thrust of a waterfall we were swimming behind in Hava Supai canyon; rehydrated us in the altitude and switch-backs of Mount Whitney. She is an Amazon and at the same time fully feminine. I would trust her to reach into a uterus and pull out a reluctant fetus, and if I were the fetus, I would trust her enough to be born.

Mo tells us that we should make our way to shore for lunch in order to get back in time for any school pick-ups. She is the hub of our wheel, the one to keep our contacts fresh and current. She knows the best gossip, but she doesn't (usually) tell. She is one of the size two's, yet her shoulders have been plenty broad enough to lovingly bear many tears. She and Melissa are the "M & M" who plan our infamous Christmas parties, ranging from a videotaped team scavenger hunt through two towns, to flag football, to a progressive dinner on bicycle (only one minimally bloody wipe-out that night). Her laughter has many times incited me to happily escalate inappropriate humor.

We are missing Melissa today, as she could not take the day off work as she thought she could.

The mojitos, however, represent her, as they are her gift on ice to us, sent on through a friend. She calls me when she needs a quick answer to something I know anything about. Her trust in me makes me reach for my best self. She has survived more than anyone should be asked to survive, yet keeps moving forward, taking along those who depend upon her, adversity never allowed to steal her grace. I miss her today, and know that if she were here, we would be swimming out farther and farther at her athletic insistence.

There will be photos to share after this, courtesy of Jody. So often she has been the "stoke" to our fire, inspiring and guiding active trips to parts we would have left unexplored but for her: the Grand Canyon, Yosemite, Zion. We call her Ranger Jo. I feel as if I have watched her grow up these years, even though chronologically she is not far behind me. Currently she is rangering her parents through to another destination these days, far from this world, stepping up as both child and adult. Both her kids have now moved out, and she and her husband have snugly feathered their own empty nest with love, inspiring and amusing those of us with kids still at home.

We are changing, my friends and I. Like this beach, we were once overrun with kids, our own rhythms dictated by their urgencies. Not so very long before that we were the children ourselves. Different faces, different seasons, different sounds on the breeze. But the tantalizing color of the water here is the same it has always been, the sand just the same radiant shade of white. Is our own beauty not unlike this? Is it changed by perspective and time, but in its essence just as brilliant?

Whatever we started out to be has been reworked. On the way to plans we may have once plotted as young women, we took detours: we gave what needed to be given, we sacrificed what we needed to sacrifice in order to take care of what needed to be taken care of. We had to let go of what we were planning to be in order to become what we were becoming. We had to let go of the children we had planned to raise in order to embrace the children we actually had. We sometimes lay buried for a while after we were broken, scarcely able to fill our lungs with breath, obscured from the light by our pain, or our embarrassment and shame at thinking we were the only ones fractured. But each time we resurfaced, many times pulled up by the mighty unshakeable grip of a friend or two. Or ten.

The sea glass we will find here is some of the best around, of many colors, most ready for the taking. The generations who used this sand long before we arrived, a bit sloppy about their empty bottles, have aided us: some of the shards harken back many decades.

Were we to pick the colors representing each of ourselves, which would we choose? Common green, brown, and white? I don't think so. Likely the more rare citron, aqua, teal and yellow. Certainly amethyst, as it is the name of a jewel, and hides some of its elemental composition from the casual examiner, revealed only in a dark room under a special light. I choose elusive orange for myself, as it is related to carnivals and rainbow effects, and Frank Sinatra said it is the happiest color.

We unearth our treasure, and it is us: different than what we once were, both in form and purpose, surprising, refashioned. Together. Each of us has been broken by the inscrutable relentless tides of life, but we were not destroyed. Far from it. We took what aimed to break us, and claimed it. We are strong like beach glass, transforming what is left after being shattered into the singular and precious beauty shaped by surviving.

•7•
Strands

We have survived the tsunami warning from an earthquake in Chili. Its tragedy did not result in destruction here, but rather in waves just fierce enough to excite the surfers now slicing them into triangles and quadrangles with their boards. The tides have been dramatic, however, and today it is as if the Seven Chinese Brothers have stepped out of their fable, and the brother thus talented has indeed swallowed the sea. I am the youngest brother, scampering out to rarely accessible spots to scoop up treasures newly revealed by this extreme low tide.

The beach has been scrubbed raw. Big waves have scoured away all the cushioning sand from the pockets it had previously filled. Rocks and boulders usually buried up to their tips lay exposed, as if Strands' gigantic exoskeleton has been set upon by piranhas, or cannibals. This new lunar landscape is as far removed from turquoise summer days as Anchorage is from Miami. In the rocks, striations and depictions of mineral composition appear that I have never seen before. At the base of an access ramp typically anchored in the sand, but now suspended one foot above it, a rock shockingly presents a perfect fossilized scallop shell, the upper half of Botticelli's Birth of Venus.

This whole area, like the rest of the country and much of the world, has survived – is surviving – its own recent financial tsunami, too, and we wait to see how our new landscape will look. What seemed like truthful bedrock has proved to be not so, and we realize now that math, in finances as it was also proved in elementary school, is less about "new" than about basics. Multiplying x by y in order to subtract z only holds its center as long as both sides of the equation continue to make sense. We will look back on this time as changing some people's equations irrevocably. Even in this affluent "bubble" of South Orange County things have changed, and "upside down" is no longer just for monkey bars. My daughters each have friends whose families have relocated near or far out of necessity, or made shifts to less rather than more. If one has the cash, this is a great time to buy oceanfront dirt.

Like this scraped winter beach, I am raw myself, carrying my own gray cloudy secret. I have not figured out how to carry it in my hands, or how to share it, or how to quite look at it, even, so it is tucked away in my pack, where its weight presses at my back.

I have reached the middle of the beach, sufficiently distanced from the small crowd at the surf point to claim my own patch of ocean, sky and sand. The deep breath I can only now take in surprises me with its ragged edges, as if I have been running hard, or crying. I have done neither, but the creaky lobes of my lungs now expanding with air inform me how shallowly I must have been breathing for some time, like a beast trying to outrun a predator. Something scratchy in me is both full and hollow at the same time, and I am yet unequipped to call its name.

Today is Sunday. Tomorrow my oldest daughter will leave our house at 3:45am to catch a ride to a processing center in Los Angeles where she will take any number of physical and psychological tests. At the end of the hours of these tests, if she passes them, she will raise her right hand and swear into the United States Army and sign a binding five-year contract. For the last three weeks she has talked about this idea, and the recruiter she met near her school campus, and the great jobs for which her aptitude test scores to date qualify her. She has recently moved home after a year and a bit away, an awkward and difficult year for all of us, and I have seen this as a twenty-year-old's fleeting exploration of options with a dash of rebellion thrown in, nothing more. (Ironic that in South Orange County joining the military is seen as rebellion, but this is definitely land of the college-bound, and most of our offspring here aim to that end as unquestioningly as summer does to fall.)

The sea must be female, I decide, as she folds me into her cadence while I walk. The crash of each wave and its suck back out to sea following the wave before it and the wave before that comforts me, as if to soothe my frayed arrhythmia into step with her beating heart, the same as I calmed my children's nightmare breaths into tempo with my own by holding them in the night and stroking their hair, loving them back to safe sleep.

Why does parenting so often find me one step too slow? How is it that my daughters reach a destination so much quicker than I do, and step blithely off my platform into the stations of their own life dreams and plans before I have quite completed my intentions with them? I am still proceeding full speed ahead on one rail, and they have pulled the signal and disembarked, or changed routes, before I have even slowed.

I fear that my oldest has suffered this parental time lag the most, as my husband and I only just became parents with her, before we had even the portion of humility that we have now earned. We learned lessons via our experiences with her that benefited her sisters, yet too often came late for her. By merit of her spot in our family, she has nearly always been the first to reach a stage, and so it still is today. Foolish me, I had thought her true launch into adulthood was still years off. How naïve; at her age I certainly considered myself an adult. Yet, especially with her move back home, I thought we had pushed the "restart" button, that we would all get a chance to reform our relationships with greater wisdom and gentleness. I had thought she would get another chance to restart the leg of the same journey that had ended up causing her pain and confusion. But I am now learning (again) that there is no such thing as restarting the same journey; each day, and each choice brings us to a fresh jump off point, and there is no going back.

The largest shard in my pocket draws my fingers to its one slightly sharp corner. Technically, I shouldn't keep it, but I have held onto it, as it is an elusive curved piece, perhaps initially the punt of a wine bottle, and I want it. Broken once, and then broken again, its journey towards smooth beauty has not been direct, doubling back upon itself, yielding its form more than once to the ocean's tumbling.

I meander up to the boulders again, away

from the shore break where I scooped up this Chinese Brother treasure. It is the rocks that most fascinate me today, as if I have never noticed them before. And indeed, eighty percent of what I see of them I have not ever been able to see, because the sand had always covered it.

A huge rock like Saturn sits naked ahead, its white rings imbedded in its black surface. I am the crowd of scientists who have studied it as I approach and learn more with each advancing step: Galileo first spotting it, Huygens discovering its thin flat ring, Cassini finding that the ring was actually "rings," and that there is a division between them. Now I am NASA, discovering that the rings are made of water ice, composed of braids and ringlets, and spokes within rings, which circle the planet at rates different than even the ring that contains them.

The boulder unfolds its mysteries as I step nearer. It has not changed its composition just because I was not able to see it or fathom it. Nor has this latest storm changed the character of this rock, merely revealed it. It has not changed at all; it is my capability to see it that has changed.

Now my ragged breaths do tell of tears. My daughter is leaving me. She has always been leaving me, but I just couldn't see it. I am afraid and nervous for her, I am not done with her, and I have not told her "I love you" enough. But she is leaving anyway. No matter how much I love her, I am her past, and she must step away from me into her future. This is as it should be. I am broken. I am breaking. The heavy lump in my pack begins to take a form, and I know that the sea is giving me strength to find a way to hold it.

I have always been proud of my child, and very many times surprised by her. She is the strong-willed person who informed me that what she most wanted upon her ninth or tenth birthday was for the rest of us to leave her the house for the weekend alone. She hadn't planned any wild pre-pubescent parties, but just wanted to have the house to herself. This child learned to ride a bike in one long day, back and forth across the backyard lawn, falling and rising to try again until she was sweaty and red-faced, and she could do it. In seventh grade, when she wanted a 70's style bikini, she took apart one she found, taught herself to crochet and made her own. Then she made ten more and sold those to her friends. She has never felt at home among the affluence that surrounds us here, and disdains with undisguised contempt what she perceives as an entitled attitude. She loves to work hard, craves significance, and never wants to sit at the children's table. This child has been chasing adulthood for so long already.

When she first left my body at birth, I shook and shivered at night for days, sweating myself into a new equilibrium without her inside me. I was excited to have her leave my womb, thought I was ready, yet the process still shocked me. The void she left happened naturally, though her physical absence left my body almost violently up-set. And it was I who had to adjust to a lack of her where she had been -- she slept and ate and cried and pooped, just as she should have, just as she was designed to do. It was I who had to find a new way to wrap myself around the reality of where she was and where she was not. She did her job, and I had to learn how to do my own.

My daughter is a planet unfolding itself to those who see her, who would thoughtfully observe her, yet what she is made of is already in place. The sand around her will surely ebb and flow, and she will certainly find herself scraped raw by dramatic turns in the tide. But the storms ahead will serve to reveal her character to herself and leave behind them a treasure for her to discover: her own bedrock. She has launched herself into her own future, and this is her time.

I pitch the yet jagged shard as far back out to sea as I can throw it. Broken once, and broken again, it must still be broken again. My child is doing her job, and I must find a way to do my own.

• 8 •
Kanaka Bay

I am the beneficiary of sound real estate plans made by others. The twenty-acre property where I reside abuts a 100-acre property overlooking the cold Northwest Pacific, blue and wild and fresh. All 120 generous acres are usually mine alone, however, as I housesit "my" own parcel this winter, and trespass through a split rail fence nearly daily onto this next estate owned by a Seattle family with a famous name who rarely come here. When they do, it is by airplane, landing on their own airstrip, thereby kindly giving me plenty of noisy notice to stay away.

I love their house, frankly offering its honest symmetrical face west to the sea and the sunset, its wide porch decorated organically with red berry branches and shells, smooth rocks and cottony pieces of cedar driftwood. I admire but do not touch the remnants of others' foraging days; the meandering, picking up, putting down, pocketing and the later laying out of treasures this island requires is so personal that disturbing the fruit of another's discovery and sorting would be like snooping into a private diary. The house is a perfect size, I think: two wings of bedrooms radiating up and out from the huge great room with a kitchen at its back, all oriented to the sea. Broad steps run its length, inviting and expecting a sit, a hiatus, a long look out to water and horizon. The orca pods can often be seen hunting here, or making love, or doing whatever they do in the moments of their everyday life they choose to share as they break the whitecaps with their loud breath.

Clean air bright with essence of sea lettuce and kelp, otter and urchin gusts through my brain here, taking every cobweb prisoner without quarter, ushering it to a swift execution. I hardly know this oxygenated version of myself, every day filled more with her in this place so truly mine I cannot help but wonder that I didn't spring up here like one of the wild blackberry bushes full of both fruit and thorns.

I have come here this winter by myself, taking the final step in a series of serendipitous dog-legs that led me to packing my old VW bug, driving north to a house I had never seen, and de-camping to housesit for an indefinite number of months. I left behind an incipient career as a high school teacher, quitting after my first year. I load-ed a smallish storage unit with boxes of stuff, paid my bills six months ahead, and drove away from the man I am contemplating marrying...or not. My head is full of static crackle and unanswered questions, and full of all of what school and work has pounded into it. I expected something dif-ferent from myself at this point, and find myself confused, knowing less of what I say yes to, than of what I say no to. Is this what I became when I grew up? I drew a line of my life, and did not envi-sion this break in it, but at 25, I have moved into a pause, a caught breath, a fermata island of time, playing it out here surrounded by water and tall trees, many miles away from what I left behind.

The late afternoon of my arrival day here, a cacophony drew me outside my strong pine house to a huge tree covered in red berries. It had filled with birds, each squawking, gorging itself. The whole of them created a din of a sound I had never heard before. I watched as the blue-black birds denuded the tree, flying away after reducing it to a silent Japanese ink sketch of itself. It was full of fruit when I drove up and busily let myself into the cold unfamiliar house, followed all the entry directions, and unpacked my bags and notebooks, my juicer and my expectations. In a few hours, however, the birds arrived and stripped it bare, then flew away engorged, leaving not a single red berry.

Normal birds in a normal day for them, I guessed, yet my first in a long string of before and after moments here. If I had arrived one day, or even a few hours later, I would have missed it all, yet the island simply flipped the singular experience to me, just like that, a casual overflow splash of its bounty of surprising tides. It caught my attention as freshly as a slap delivering me from my busyness, reading like a warning label on the bottle of this island: Will Not Conform to Expectations.

Like so many travelers, I packed too much. I have brought too much of an old me onto this island, but am every day divesting. Most of my clothes get returned to my bag, leaving me a daily outfit that becomes my uniform: old too-big jacket given me by my father as an afterthought when I visited him on my way up the western coast; high black muck boots bought in a WalMart, also on my way here; jeans tucked into boots; shirt; red neck scarf. Sometimes a hat. The island is plucking my old layers from me as surely as berries from a tree, insisting upon its own version of me, teaching me to simplify, strip distractions, breathe deeply. Wearing the same thing every day frees up brain cells needed to make new choices every 24 hours.

My daily routine is simple, too, as quickly skinned of my earnest expectations as my wardrobe from my back: I rise, I walk, I think, I write, I read, I walk. I eat, and sometimes I drive to town, or to another side of the island. Mostly I walk, and I think, and I breathe. I write a lot less than I thought I would. On my walk to the mailbox a mile out the dirt road, I sometimes leave my jacket on a branch in the warming sun, picking it up on my way back. I sing out loud if I want to. At night, I dream wild dreams, tangled dreams that sometimes leave me sweating or weeping. I dream of cutting my way upward through a forest of kelp between me and the surface of the ocean, able to see the sky through the water, aware that I need to reach the air. The man I left behind hands me helpful unfamiliar tools underwater in this dream, but I must do all the cutting work myself. I don't really do much here, yet my days are full.

I also walk to Kanaka Bay, the nearest shoreline. Its rocks are sharp with gooseneck barnacles and slippery with green seaweeds. Kelp here grows huge, thick stems trailing enormous bulbs at their termini, brazenly evidencing the fertility of these waters. Deep beneath my feet somewhere placidly live and breathe the geoduck clams, hinting at their silent existence below by the rims of their siphons dimpling the wet sand. They like me because I am too lazy to shovel them up, preferring a drive to Westcott Bay and a purchase to a sandy wet sucky dig.

I don't see many humans, but I do have one friend. A sea otter watches me from the ocean, shadowing me in my walks along the shore. He does not hide his examination of me, like we humans do as we check each other out. He stares right at me. He flips over and back, and then he stares at me some more. He is agile and funny without trying. He is curious. He must live in this bay, as he appears nearly every time I walk down. I think we are getting to know one another, building a friendship of sorts. I pick about, turning over this rock, this shell, this bit of driftwood, and he watches me, chewing on things, shaking water out of his eyes, flipping onto his back. Sometimes I simply sit and look at him and the sea and the horizon, smoothing a tumbled pebble in my fingers like a rosary, sorting my thoughts into piles as the sun warms my back. We are each about our work.

I have found more shorelines on the island, each flavored uniquely: Roche Harbor, Lime Kiln, American Camp. Each faces a different compass point, so is therefore less or more sunny, less or more exposed to the waves. Cedar driftwood lines nearly all the shores, pummeled into cottony shapes with rounded ends, perfect for splintering into the kindling my two house stoves crave ravenously. Small beach pebbles here invite one into their world like an Aladdin's trove: colors, shapes, embedded stripes to be scooped and sifted by the handful, slipping through my fingers like silk. I have amassed one small pile that all look like sunflower seeds, and another pile shaped like hearts. I found a tree with a huge twig nest, lived in season after season by a great bald eagle, politically protected from ever losing its home. I am amazed by this island and its embrace of me. I explore as much of it as I can, but I always return to Kanaka Bay, for it is my beach, and my friend awaits me there.

As my months progress, the winter turns colder. I have learned the art of woodstove, building fires that can actually last through the night. I keep the biggest stove going most faithfully, sometimes neglecting the other. I reduce my house time mainly to the huge bathroom suite the big stove occupies; I think it must have originally been the full bedroom for its size. I take my books there, making forays into the kitchen and up to my bedroom when it is time, diving under the heavy down comforter, grateful for my bed's position directly above the workhorse stove.

I read and read, write letters, sit and think and watch the trees outside my windows. I leave my jacket less frequently when I walk, yet still make my way down to the Bay. I hear of an approaching "Siberian Blast," which reportedly is bringing freezing temperatures, high winds, and threats to all the docks in Friday Harbor. I am advised to lay in food, water and wood, and to not count on electricity or plumbing for a while.

Days and nights coldly run into each other, bringing snow when the Blast does hit, an amazing snow that dusts the tops of all branches, and turns the landlocked old truck I walk past every day into a postcard. I stay close to home, surviving frozen plumbing with the help of the home's original outhouse, braving nights that are noisy with wind-pummeled pine trees, sitting closer and closer to my stove, until I just can't take it anymore and check into a town hotel, unwinding my cold tense muscles there by a wall heater that works like a champ.

Wind chill drives the temperature well below freezing. Seventeen boats are lost from the docks, and the forecast says that although the worst is past, we are still in for a lot more of a long hard winter. I haven't been to the shore for days.

Finally the weather breaks, a bit, and I walk down to the bay. The sky is a frothy cake top of frozen white clouds, still and foreboding. I am walking down to say goodbye, as my time is done here, hurried to its completion by the cold. The new owners of the house I live in actually needed me less than they thought, and will complete the first winter of this house's ownership without me. The owners of my "second" home at the shore remain unaware of their squatter, and I believe I have swept away all my tracks there.

I am not taking much of my physical discoveries away with me; indeed, I have returned most to the woods and am carrying the rest with me now to throw back into the sea. But the pockets of my heart are full: I have learned to build a fire, and decided that I am too young to teach high school. I learned to sit and watch whales and to thank them for the window they opened to me. I can cook a geoduck and eat it alone.

I have become part of an island, and I have a sea otter friend. I have found that part of myself that is not the net result of the world's input, but instead the still part of myself that contents itself alone. I have found the "yes" I will deliver when I get home. I am glass and I am pebble, tumbled by this island, rich with it.

• 9 •
San Roque

We are three families with kids, two still in diapers; one newly married couple without kids; and my husband's friend, Donny, who serves as our informal experienced guide into a part of Baja California, Mexico we have not visited before. Days and nights spent in travel and detours, some of which were intentional, have brought the 14 of us to the wide-open bay of San Roque. We set up camp at the north end, allowing the sweep of the bay to stretch away from us like a flamenco dancer's turned hand. A small seasonal fishermen's settlement sits behind us, the panga boats lined up before it at the ready for their morning forays.

Our camp bears testament to the joy of our

men in creating something out of nothing. They are quintessentially male here: providing for their families in the most primal terms. I realize now that what I first saw as worrisome problems on our early Baja trips – mechanical vehicle problems, an imperative to create shade out of the harsh Baja sun, keeping at least some sand out of the tents – represent opportunities for my husband and his male friends to reclaim the ingenuity and resourcefulness of their pioneer predecessors. They have been camping throughout Baja since they were teenagers: surfing, diving, fishing. Off the beaten path, these men rediscover the part of themselves called into being by necessity: create it, or go without.

Our current camp demonstrates this mindset in high art form: we enjoy easily-swept "porches" outside our tents of foraged empty clamshells embedded edge-side down into the sand, and our shade canopy is an ephemeral art installation of blue tarps, bungee cords, and Mexican serape blankets that get repositioned strategically according to the movements of the sun. The resourceful Baja attitude is infectious, with all of us, including the kids, joining in to invent and repurpose what we find. (On the way home from this trip, we will be stopped by fried wiring under the hood of our truck, chewed on by a beach rat who had settled in as we camp, and met his end via electrocution when we started up the truck again. That problem will be fixed by a young Mexican mechanic under a palapa, who asks $20 for a repair that would cost us many hundreds stateside.)

We eat simply and luxuriously, nearly every dish emanating from the same fresh salty waters providing us kayak and swimming fun, the billion-dollar view and our nightly lullaby. Our camp boat and kayaks go out every day, each of the fishermen and divers excited to be commissioned with the job of feeding such a large group. Their recreation is our sustenance, both sides content with this arrangement. To the daily haul from the sea, we add what we purchased at El Gigante, the Mexican supermarket we hit before heading off road: cabbage and tomatoes that we chop, fresh farmer's cheese, toasted handmade tortillas, limes, and copious amounts of hot sauce. Because our loyalties diverge, the tables provide an egalitarian slate of options with which we singe our tastebuds: Tapatío, Búfalo, Cholula. One night we make a sumptuous Baja gumbo, rich with abalone, lobster, rock cod and cabrilla. We add the file powder we packed, dancing as we cook, sipping cold Pacífico beers brightened with squeezed limes. The chocolate we brought along is scarce and sweet in contrast to the other flavors of this camp food making it a rare treasure to be parceled out and savored.

Fresh gastronomic hedonism becomes second nature here, and we are pleased to see the children eating nothing processed. "Fast food" in San Roque means ten minutes from ocean to plate, and our kids adjust instantly. Upon returning to California, one of our young daughters will innocently order abalone in a restaurant, which in her mind is simply something delicious she ate naked, not something rare or posh.

Our hair and our skin wear that slightly crunchy stretched feeling of washing and rinsing in the ocean, swimming in it all day, washing our dishes at its edge and returning our scraps to its crabs. We wear it, we wash in it, we eat from it.

My blood stream's salinity rises, my fluids in the process of being flushed and replaced with pelagic brine. Our pillows smell like campfires, and "clean" takes on new shades of relative meaning.

We rise with the sun, some of us sleeping outdoors under the tarp. My early-girl baby rolls to her elbows each morning, watching out the camper window as the dark indigo sky flames pink and orange, and the stars change places with the sun. The warm breeze choreographed to split night from dawn stirs this transition, beginning its movement with the dawning light.

During the day, the kids casually leave their clothes wherever they need to drop them in order to take part in the newest Roxaboxen recreation of the moment. They run back and forth from the water to the camp, enjoying the liberty a bay of only small lapping waves affords them. They have carved "stores" into the crusty berm, stocking their driftwood shelves with prized coffee beans, cowries, Chinamen's hats, seaweed, and other oceanic mercantile. They trade amongst themselves, chattering for hours, a happy tribe of sandy sticky citizens of the beach, shedding civilization and donning suntans in a blissful exchange. We will take home brown skin and sandy sleeping bags, but also the sunshine and abandon we have stored up during this vacation.

Without our saying so, I know that as parents, each of us is treasuring these moments in San Roque. Some of what is confusing and complicated at home smoothes out in this place. Naked kids running until they drop, sleeping until they are rested, eating until they are full, is simple and tangible here. Laughter comes easily on this beach, and just living is our entertainment. We share a communal innocence here.

At home, we are daily growing up along with our kids, sometimes feeling too much of the weight of our adult responsibility for these little people. At this point, none of us have faced major challenges with our children: none of them have turned into teenagers; none have suffered major illness or even heartbreak. The "problems" we suffer revolve around babies sleeping through the night, diaper rash, preschools and talking back. Nonetheless, we feel the growing significance of our actions in the lives of these children, and fall breathless sometimes with the importance of it. We will need the easy moments stockpiled here to draw upon later.

Currents ahead will shift in our lives, of which we are still unaware. Among the families here, still waiting to be born in surging tides coming are five more girls and two boys (one girl child conceived on this very trip). Our friend Tom, author of so many of our adventures, and master of the jerry-rigged kayak sail, will leave us too soon at the age of 51. And, in an especially excruciating ebb tide, one of these beautiful baby girls will have grown into a stunning young woman full of poems and dreams but be taken from the lot of us when her head lands wrong in an epileptic seizure at the age of 19.

Our innocence will run away willfully through our clenched fingers, as surely as sand flushed by sea. The precious young people entrusted to us will move away from us, out of the protective reach of our arms. We will want to hold onto each one to keep them safe, but we will not be able to. Inevitably, holding onto them will prove as futile as holding onto laughter, or sunshine, the Baja sand or a certain shade of tan. Still, we will attempt to clutch tighter and tighter as storms rage, clenching them into ourselves like precious glass vessels we are meant to preserve whole. Weren't we meant to? There were many aspects to parenting that confused us, but that one seemed clear: hold on with all your might and keep those little people safe. But they changed in our arms and holding on was not possible. Wrenched from our grasps like glass bottles in a storm, sometimes they broke, and the cuts left to us ran deeper than could have been imagined. What we loved will be ripped from us outright. We will discover that we can die and yet live.

We will transform and endure. Somehow, we will survive agonizing adversity, but we will pay for our transformations with our very wholeness. Shattered, buffeted, confused and cut deeply, we are to be sometimes left without the slightest semblance of simplicity or explanation. Ahead of us, we will seek answers and find none. We will not know what to say to another of us to provide any meaningful comfort at all and will be made to settle for merely accompanying each other through the storms and aftermath, dabbing at each other's wounds with only our presence as poultice. We will love each other, and we will accept what comes, after a time, but we will not see any treasure worth the loss it required.

We will reflect back on our days on this beach, at the beginning of so much we could not have known was coming. In our beginnings there, were endings, too. Our treasures incorporated unseen losses, too. We would find shadows behind the light, cracks in what we thought unbreakable, and the innocence of our unawareness was to be swept from us like sand from a tent.

• 10 •
Three Arch Bay

The very north end of the crescent shore of this private beach terminates at Whale Rock, the huge sedimentary rock mammal with its head pointed out to sea, its tail creating tidepools and kid-sized cliffs. Where its huge "head" dives down to meet its "tail" you can find the three arches that give this bay its name: three passageways between the tidepools of Whale Rock and Shell Beach, the small cove around the corner, which hews to flavors of Carmel and Monterey in its more windward presentation to the open ocean. Whether you will be able to walk through or see through all the arches depends on the season and the tide, as sometimes they are one, two or three flooded to pedestrians, while at other times they are welcoming keyholes to run through and explore.

I have tried many times to quantify the colors of Three Arch Bay, wanting to translate its hues into home decor: indigo of mussel shell; blush or apricot or flame of sky; putty fading to buff of sand; white of bleached coral fronds. But I'm left with just a handful of ambition, as Three Arch Bay refuses translation; she will not be transported anywhere but my heart and imagination. She is synergy and alchemy, impossible to unwind strand by strand.

I walked this beach as a single young woman, falling in love with the man who introduced me to it. I walked it at night after quarreling with him when we lived here. I walked it pregnant with each of our babies, then later soothing those babies from their crankiness with the rhythm of my steps in the sand, and the constancy of the waves lapping the shore. Our daughters joined two generations before them in eating the sand here, and when they got older, their shrieks punctuated their race from the waves nipping at their feet. When they grew old enough to dive under the tiny waves nearest shore, they ran back to me to check in: "Did you see that one? Did you see me?" This beach has drawn a clear line, strong yet gentle, through all our lives.

I know this place in every mood and season. In the summer she is soft, fat with sand, inviting divers under her aqua waves and warm gentle swells. In the winter, she is fierce: historical photos attest to the reality that hard-angled breakers have cracked high enough to nearly reach the windows of the southernmost and northernmost cliffside homes. Autumn and spring shoulder these two other seasons with secret morning fog, and an empty curved crescent beach in transition. Independence Day and Labor Day bookend summer, turning a walk with my husband into a crowded small town parade as he delightedly greets old friends who come back for these holidays, some not seen for years, bringing their own kids and turning us all back into happy children.

Nature herself helped create this private community, forming the only truly private access beach along this stretch of coastline by dint of cliffs at both ends. It has been claimed in succession by Native Americans, then tomato farmers, then summer campers, then 1940s movie stars who built homes here to go on vacation, but still stay within their two-hour Hollywood call zone. The biggest boom came with families venturing south from Los Angeles or Pasadena to build their own board-and-batten summer houses. Presently, the few remaining original cottages and fully-grown trees coexist with striking mansions and postcard views. I have chatted on this beach with high-powered entrepreneurs and people famous to the world, but more often with adults my husband grew up with.

My dear "mother-in-love," Meta, discovered Three Arch Bay in the late 1950s, determined to raise her babies on the beach, as she put it. She and her handsome young husband, Bob, bought a lot on the ocean side of the highway for $5000 and built a simple midcentury modern house on it for $25,000. She designed it and he helped build it, cementing the smooth stones brought load by load from Doheny into broad winding stair steps up to the front door. My husband nearly lost his life as a toddler when he crawled out onto the skeleton of

115

the house under construction, but thankfully his four-year-old brother tugged him back off the second story to safety. The house was even featured in Sunset Magazine in the early 1960s, Meta and Bob photographed on those steps with their summer buzz cut boys.

They raised three boys and a girl in this Bay, Brook coming ten years after the third brother was born. The stories of the sixties and seventies here are Dennis the Menace raucous and Mayberry innocent, full of lemon wars and street football games, painted Easter bunny footprints down the stairs to sandy egg hunts, and towheaded school bus stop line ups. Lots of parties where the parents smoked and drank, played cards and laughed, and the kids wandered between houses, eating out of whichever refrigerator was handy. The filter of years has softened the hard edges of divorces and illness, alcoholism, troubled kids and financial worries, but of course those were there as well.

As the world discovered Laguna Beach, property values skyrocketed, which altered the flavor of Three Arch Bay, bringing in quite a few Joneses to keep up with, complicating the simplicity of early years. The house my husband grew up in was sold, remodeled, and raised a new family, which has created its own decades of memories. We live nearby, our continued precious access granted via the generosity of family friends who now own here.

How shockingly quickly our days of toting three kids here passed, twisted in a kaleidoscope of wrinkled time, when hours with babies sometimes took forever, but whole years telescoped too fast into themselves. Now we travel much lighter, just the two of us. No more prized bounty of sea treasures and grains of sand emptied from pockets and shoes at our back door. This man's hand around mine has remained constant through the years, though: still strong and sweet. We have talked and walked out many things here, the cadence of our steps carding them smooth like the brambles from wool. This home beach holds so many of our words, and also more than a few of my tears. Salt water to salt water, like unto like.

Ten years ago, a new chapter opened up for us with the acquisition of two dogs. A classic dog story, in that we set out to get one dog for a daughter turning fifteen. She did all the research and found a litter of rescue pups available for adoption, and we put in our long application, getting approved to come pick out the one she wanted. How we ended up bringing home two is family lore now, but certainly involves me trying to sway her choice away from the runt to the one I considered cuter at that first meeting.

So we brought home two, sisters but not twins, one black and one gray. As if to school me in the error of my first impression, that runt, named Ruthie, quickly and decisively adopted me, and soon followed me step by step throughout my day. Although smaller, she dominated her sister, Lola, both physically and intellectually. In later years both dogs stayed behind as each of their girls moved out; by then Ruthie's allegiance had clearly transferred to me and there was never any question about her staying. In the years when sleep withdrew its easy friendship from me, Ruthie would always rise, too, cuddling my feet on the couch while I read. In the car, she also stayed close. It was probably foolish and unsafe, but we figured out a way for her to ride on my lap as I drove, somehow nestled in like water around a stone. If Wade traveled, she rightly assumed that she would be allowed to sleep on our bed with me, and up she hopped at bedtime. Many times in the wee hours, even when he was also in the bed, I would hear her little paw scratching gently at my side, delicately waiting for my forthcoming permission to jump up and find a spot behind my knees or at my belly.

At the beach, Ruthie and Lola showed us what pure joy looks like: so excited running down the south stairs that they yelped all the way, ending with a leap and an uncontainable tumble at the bottom, squabbling and rolling before tearing off down the beach.

Dog owners at the Bay may not know each

other's names, but we know each other's dogs. We don't ask or really care what the humans "do." Thankfully, it's no cocktail party. But we know all about the dogs: Chloe is aggressive, Mindy is angelic, Monster is a face licker. Spitty tennis balls get shared, bottoms sniffed, and various degrees of friendliness displayed. It's funny how some days all the dogs are black, or tan, or on another day almost all are the same breed (Labradoodles currently du jour, replacing golden retrievers and "purse dogs" before that). We are the morning crew, defying leash laws and pushing against the end time of our morning curfew hour.

Lola and Ruthie took their own place in this community, too. In a dog crowd, Lola unfortunately revealed a nature submissive to a fault: always the humpee. She was happiest leaving any canine group, while Ruthie loved to interact and incite other dogs to pursue her. Mostly they operated as a unit of two, and their beach fun meant running and chasing birds, digging enthusiastically, and hunting squirrels up the hills, fast on the trail of a squeak. Always the running, multiplying the beach's quarter mile stretch many times over in a day. Both sprinted fast enough that people stopped and watched them, as they strained into speed so hard that their bodies, especially Ruthie's, lowered and stretched, galloping like horses. Typically they would sprint for a measure, slow to a lope or walk, come back to check in with us, maybe dig a little, then be off again as a pair. This went on the whole time we walked, their ten steps to our one, culminating with tired dogs slowly climbing the stairs to go home, Ruthie especially exhausted after keeping up with Lola's longer stride all morning.

One morning, we extended our departure time particularly late. The sun on the wet sand glittered. A soft breeze tempered the sun's rising heat. The beach had pretty much emptied of dogs and their owners, and the day beachgoers had not yet encamped, which gave our two dogs full rein. They had played hard the whole time, hunting squirrels and birds, digging and chasing balls, running on and on. Lola finally ambled off on her own up the dry sand ahead of us, digging at something only she could smell. But Ruthie continued running, capturing my attention.

Her stride lengthened smoothly, as she leaned rhythmically into her run. Her body looked simultaneously relaxed and fully engaged. Up and back she loped alone in the surf line, sketching wide curves with her path. In contrast to her usual attachment, she didn't look back at her humans at all. She looked out to sea, or straight ahead. She didn't even check in with her sister. She appeared to be blissfully alone in her moment. Who knows what a dog thinks, but to me, it suddenly appeared that she wasn't running after anything, but rather running as an end in itself, spirit and body fully integrated. In that flash, she somehow seemed less to me like a dog on a beach, than simply another live entity on the earth.

I have found that most wonderful moments that become treasured memories later do so only upon reflection. Or sometimes only upon looking through photographs. They pass, and then I reach back for them, only later realizing how really good they were. While they are happening it is so rare to look up and recognize that "this is the good stuff." But in that instant on the beach, I did become aware. On that ordinary morning, on that sand, just for a blink, time seemed to stop. For a few exquisite timeless minutes, I recognized this rarity: someone truly in her bliss, fully happy, fully exerted, beyond thought. This moment was hers, and mine to bear witness to her.

At the end of our time on the beach that day, Ruthie climbed the south stairs very slowly, taking each one paw by paw. She did make it up by herself but had to be lifted into the truck. She slept the rest of the day. Clearly, she had poured herself out onto the sand completely.

Ruthie left us not so long after this. One morning, instead of hopping up into the truck to drive down to the beach, she instead sprinted up our street. She was full of energy and mischief after a few rainy days of confinement. I am deeply sorry to say that I had let her off her leash. She was sprinting so fast that when she turned left to come back to us her momentum carried her into the street just as a car rounded the corner. Neither was able to stop, and my special little friend passed away in my arms, exhaling one deep last breath as she surrendered into me. I will never forget the horror of that morning, but neither the deep sad sweetness of it, grateful to have been there and hold her as she passed. Grief crashed hard but at least there were no unanswered questions, no note on the door, no dog that simply didn't come home.

I didn't know the magnitude of losing a dog like Ruthie...until I knew. What a pure gift she was, truly a complete person in my life, although she was a so-called pet. After she died, I realized that over her ten years with us, I had spent more time with her than with any of my kids, and that, in the simplicity of a dog's love, she'd given me a lot less heartache.

The generous sea has gifted me abundantly over the years. My jars are full of abalone shards, turban and coffee bean shells. My home spills over with multicolored beach glass tumbled smooth. Driftwood adorns my tables and walls. But even more than these, it is my imagination that is over-full: the seasons of light and tide changes, waves cracking and whispering, tidepools hiding worlds within them of sea anemones and tiny opal eye perch. The sea has also now gifted me the unfading snapshot of my Ruthie in full bliss, to caress like a piece of smooth beach glass kept in the pocket of my mind. I cannot hold any of these intangible things, yet they hold me. These cannot be lost, only found.

In all the stages and layers of my life, there is always the sea, containing me, revealing itself to me, and me to myself. When at last I am reduced on this earth to the elements of the sea - water, salt, minerals - I will both leave it behind and take it with me where I go after because it has shaped my soul.

Life's breaking waves and time passing have softened the scope of my greatest life ambitions, tumbled them like fresh beach glass getting its hard corners smoothed out. But this remains: these few written words given to me like a drawstring bag of summer sea treasures, and the hope to share them. Like I have done for Ruthie, will someone bear witness of me stretched to capacity in telling them?

I dream of being remembered in joy, that I climbed the last stair entirely exhausted, that I ran the good race and finished with my tongue hanging out sideways, panting and smiling. I would like to leave my foot prints behind for a moment before the tide comes in, but I know that they will ultimately fade, receding into a shimmer, re-claimed by the froth of a wave...and the wave after the wave after the wave after that.

But like all the intangible treasures gifted me by the sea, I think I will always be here. Never to be lost, only found. If I am lucky, I will have poured myself out completely, stretched into my stride, become whom I was meant to be and given what I was meant to give. And if I am supremely blessed, someone will remember me that way. I will take my spot in a long line of memories to be found on this sand, immortal and uncontainable as a sunset and a happy dog.

Creating this book was actually a group effort: the stories came about many times while I was in the company of people very special to me, and without whom I could not have observed and learned what I did. For this I deeply thank my beautiful daughters, Lena, Maria, and Rachel; and my husband, Wade. You are on every page, and in every word.

I also thank my dear "Oyster Tribe" friends, not only for their presence on the beaches of this book, but also for their immeasurable enthusiasm and support of my dream to write about it all. My siblings' enthusiasm for my book has touched my heart, as did my mother's; I am so glad she read an early draft before Alzheimer's Disease removed that capability. It means the world to me.

The book you are reading only took shape once I entered a mentorship known as The Cultivated Artist Experience, which is a branch of The Grove Center for the Arts and Media (www.thegrovecenter.org). My deep gratitude goes out to Joey O'Connor, Sherri Alden, Bob Murphy and Monty Kelso, who led us artists with their gracious knowledge of how artists tick, and who spoke into us the encouragement needed to take dreams from heads to pages (or canvas, table, theater screen, or airwaves). This book would not exist without these special individuals. I also thank my CAE co-artists, especially from Journey One; we created a synergy of "heart-and-art," and lasting deep friendships. The beautiful line art in this book was created by one such CAE artist, the amazingly talented Salem Cade (www.daisypetpaintings. com). The book itself was designed by another CAE artist, Joel Pritchard, who somehow caught the whiff of my intentions, made that tangible, and ultimately even better than I had envisioned.

Perhaps most of all, I am grateful to you, dear reader. If you have given me your precious time and read my beach glass stories, you have gifted me deeply. I would love to hear your impressions of these stories, and perhaps your own tales of beach glass...and life. Please keep in touch – find me at www. LindaBinley.com.

18794791R00072